—— THE ——
ACCELERATED METHOD

A Guide to Accelerate Manifestation of Your Desire

Written by:
Dr. Suzan Flagg Yorke

ISBN: 0615733352
ISBN 13: 9780615733357

Unless otherwise indicated, all Bible quotations are from the New King James Version, 1979, 1980, 1982, Thomas Nelson, Inc., Nashville, Tennessee.

The intent of the author is only to offer information of a general nature to help the reader in his or her quest for spiritual, mind and body empowerment. The author and the publisher assume no responsibility for the actions, or the result of such actions, of any reader, as a result of reading this book.

Ho! Everyone who thirsts,
Come *to the waters;*
And you who have no money,
Come, *buy and eat.*

Isaiah 55:1

TABLE OF CONTENTS

PREFACE

It was approximately 40 years ago when I first got the notion that you could have in life whatever you wanted. I thought that you could somehow make happen whatever it was that you desired. However, at the time I felt like a lone ranger. Most of my friends and associates did not share my belief. They called me unrealistic and idealistic. I knew in my heart that there must be a way to go about it, but I did not know what that way was. The only advice I got was that I needed to finish school, get a job, work until I was old enough to retire, and then be satisfied with whatever pension I got as retirement. By the way, that pension after working 30 years or more would only be about a fourth of the salary that was already not enough to allow me to miss a paycheck. Everything that came along the way was supposedly meant to be and there was nothing I could do to change it. What a misconception!

As I continued to seek the "Truth" of life, I began to notice that certain events or circumstances seemed to follow after I would deliberately think of them. For instance, I would think of getting a perfect parking space and would usually get one closest to the entrance of the building where I was going. Once I planned an important outdoor event, my wedding reception.

A couple of days before the reception, a ninety percent chance of heavy rain was in the forecast to hit the area on that very day. I just kept thinking that it would not rain on the day of my wedding reception. It could not rain. Everything had already been planned and set in place. All the invitations had already been sent. I did not have a plan B, in case of rain. Well, guess what? It did not rain that day. I got what I wanted. As a matter of fact, it was bright and sunny. It did downpour the next day after the reception.

Even in the area of healing, many times others have been healed and freed of pain when I would intervene on their behalf and declare healing and wholeness for them. As such events continued to happen I began to think that there must be some correlation between my thoughts and my experiences. Maybe it had to do with something in the air. Some say it had to do with my faith. I believed for certain that God was in me and I was in God.

Being a religious person, I would often pray, "Lord, teach me your way. Teach me your statutes." I prayed this prayer often for many years. I now realize that what I am learning and have learned is in answer to that prayer.

For years I studied, both formally and informally. I attended dozens of seminars, enrolled in class after class, heard countless sermons, and spent a lot of time at many spiritual retreats seeking to find out how to get what I truly wanted in life — trying to get closer to that "thing," that "good" that always seemed to elude me. I, like you may have done, read tons of books in search of what really works, in search of the truth. And although I grew and matured some, I was still not manifesting that "good" that I wanted in life. I still had no money to speak of; and I still was experiencing ill health. I still felt quite limited in my abilities. Others were still able to push my buttons. I was still bound and had not been set free.

It was one day during the early summer of 2011 when out of the blue I said, "I am going to study metaphysics." I did not have a clue at the time why I uttered such a statement. I knew nothing of what metaphysics meant, and did not know that I knew anything about Universal Laws and Principles. I did not know at the time that metaphysics simply means above and beyond the physical – involving the power of thought and the laws of Spirit. It did not occur to me at the time that what I was really saying was that I was now ready to delve deeper into the "Truths" that set men free.

Less than two years after making that statement, my life and thoughts changed in ways that I would not have imagined. I found out that you really can have what you want if you know what steps to take to make it manifest. Using what I had learned concerning the power of thought, spiritual principles, and universal laws, I designed a practical step-by-step method that has been proven to accelerate the manifestation of your desire. And I want to share that method with you.

Jesus came so that we may have "Life" and it more abundantly. Jesus said that we shall know the "Truth" and the "Truth" shall make us free. I know now that my years of seeking and my lifetime of preparation were not solely for me. It was also for you. You will not have to spend a lifetime trying to figure out how to get what you desire. The path has already been forged and the way made clear. All you have to do is follow the path — this method which is a proven approach to accelerate manifestation.

As you follow this method, this guide to life, get ready to experience what it means to live in the Kingdom of God. Get ready to experience the will of God being done on earth, as it is in heaven. Get ready to be catapulted to your desire. Get ready, my friend, and EXPERIENCE THE GOOD!

INTRODUCTION

I am convinced that there is "Good" for me, and I ought to have it. I am convinced that I really can have what I want. I am convinced that it is deception to think that I have to live a life of lack, sickness, and powerlessness. I am convinced that there is a way, a process, a breakthrough, a method that will launch me into a realm which will enable me to experience a lifestyle that now I can only dream about.

I am determined to have my "Good." I am determined to learn how to accelerate the manifestation of what I really want. I am determined to know Truth. I am determined to discover what really works. And guess what? If it works for me, it will also work for anybody and everybody else, including you.

My purpose for writing this book is twofold. First, I am writing this book as the record of a scientific experiment which proves that certain principles and laws regarding the science of mind and spirit really do and will work when properly applied. Second, I am writing this book as a practical step-by-step guidebook to help you accelerate the process of manifesting wealth, health, and power in your own life.

All my life I have seen lack, sickness, and powerlessness. One of the things that I remember most about my childhood was that no one in my family ever seemed to have enough money to really live what we called, "the good life." I had been conditioned to think that I could never have "that" because we could not afford it; or "that" was only for the rich and famous, or for those who lived on the other side of the tracks; never for me or anyone who looked like me. It seemed we were always trying to just make ends meet, living from paycheck to paycheck.

As I grew older, I started paying attention to people in general. Most people always seemed to be struggling, either with financial issues or with health issues. I have attended church most of my life, and serve in ministry. Even among those who profess faith in God, I daily witness sickness and lack being accepted as a normal and almost expected part of life. I have heard many people talk as if struggling is virtuous, saying that it must be God's will; or saying "Jesus suffered, why shouldn't I?" – Totally misinterpreting Jesus and the cross.

All around me I have been constantly bombarded with indications and suggestions of lack, sickness, disease, pain, poverty, weakness, and fear. Always wanting; always needing. Before developing and applying this method that I am about to share with you, I was 50 pounds overweight. I took medication each day to try to manage high blood pressure. I had more bills than I had paycheck. Everything was past due. My credit was at rock bottom. And I was working a job that I did not particularly love.

Still, I was convinced that there was "Good" for me and I ought to have it. The problem was that I did not know how to get it. How was I to get my "Good"? I pondered not only *how* was I to get *it*, but what was *it*? What exactly was the "Good" that I was so desperately seeking? Thus, my quest began.

I soon found out that the same stuff that I wanted was the same stuff that most other people wanted. Everyone seemed to want some measure of wealth. Most people seemed to want good health, either for themselves or for someone that they loved or knew. And everyone seemed to want some measure of power, if nothing more than to have some control and influence over their own life. Yet, I found few that had actually received the "Good" that they wanted. Most continue to live a day to day existence in the same situation with the same complacency as they had always done. Some even continue to dream; but, have never taken any persistent action to make those dreams manifest. Yet, there are a few, like yourself, who are determined to get what you want, to make a difference, to change, to find an answer, to discover what really works and apply it.

There is "Good" for you and you CAN have it. For you who want to receive the "Good" that is for you and that you ought to have, I have good news. I have discovered the way and have designed an effective method that you can easily follow which will accelerate you having "exceedingly, abundantly, above all that you ask or think."

This method teaches the use of thought power - true power of thought; not any of the substitutes and perversions. And it employs the Law of Spirit – God. It has nothing to do with hypnotism, magic or any of the more or less fascinating deceptions by which many are led to think that something can be had for nothing. It is based on proven principles and universal laws of the science of mind and spirit. When put to the test, these laws and principles have worked time and time again. They worked thousands of years ago and they work today. They have worked for others, they are working for me, and they will work for you too.

In this guidebook, you will be given a scientifically proven method which when applied, will open up a new world of manifestations for you. I chose to use a style of writing that specifically and deliberately switches between the first person and second person pronoun as a unique way of automatically engaging you, the reader, in dialogue with me and in application of this process. In addition, there are exercises throughout this guide that are designed to make both understanding and practicing the principles easier.

No longer do you have to be a "*have not*" or live a life of lack and want. No longer do you just have to accept and live with that illness or disease, regardless of the diagnosis or prognosis. No longer do you have to be powerless to effect change in your own life and in the lives of others. No longer do you have to work a lifetime hoping that someday you may get what you want. You CAN have what you want. There is "Good" for you, and YOU can have it! "*The Accelerated Method*" will guide you each step of the way to "the land of milk and honey." Are you ready to receive? Are you ready to be empowered? Let's begin by first defining the "Good."

— CHAPTER 1 —

The Good

WHAT IS THE "GOOD"?

In order for me to get *it*, I must first know and understand what *it* is. Otherwise, how will I know when I have *it*? So my first step in acquiring *it* is defining *it*. What exactly is "Good"? When I looked in the dictionary I found that the word itself could be used as an adjective, a noun or an adverb. Webster's and Wikipedia had many definitions, but, none really told me what "Good" is. They mainly gave me implications and told how I could use the word in conjunction with other words; or they tried to define it as a person, place or thing by using the word "good" to define itself. In searching the media further, I found many different implied definitions, but nothing concrete or universal. So I am still left with the question what is "Good"? What is the truth about the "Good"?

Turning to the embracement of faith, religions worldwide acknowledge that God is Good. Although, they may use different words and phrases to express it, the message is the same, God is Good. The Hindus call God "Brahman" which means: God with (good) attributes. The name "OM" was a name of God which the ancient people of Asia used to repeat during meditation. Still today, yogi and many persons when meditating repeat the word, "OM." It means: Good beyond Good. Primal religions in Africa call God "Nana" which means the Good parent. David wrote in the Psalm, "Oh taste and see that the LORD is Good."[1] God is Good. Jesus says that "No one is good but One, that is, God."[2] Throughout the history of mankind, it has been acknowledged that God, regardless of the terms used, is Good. Based on the affirmative testament of many and inductive reasoning which consists of comparing a number of separate instances with one another until the common factor which gives rise to them all is seen, God is Good.

The first name of God is Good, and the first name of the Good is God. And God is also Creator. God created and creates everything, every presence, every power; all things known and unknown. So since God is Good and Good is God; and since God is Creator, then the Good must also be Creator. Creator of what? Creator of everything. Creator of what I want. And since God – the Good, is Creator, then that which is created by the Good must also be good.

Simply put, "Good" is the name I give to what I want. It is the nearest approach to expressing my desire and what is in my mind that I have so far. God (Good) called Himself, "I AM."[3] Now the one who gets to complete that statement identifying God (Good) is me – "I AM _____."

Now that I somewhat understand what "Good" is, I need to name my "Good." In order for it to manifest I must first identify what *it* is that I want. What am I seeking? What is my desire? What is my good?

WHAT IS MY GOOD?

If I could have what I want, what would it be? What is my desire? What am I seeking? Every living creature has something that it wants. Every living creature has its Good. Ultimately, the "Good" when received leads to satisfaction and freedom. "There is Good for me," says the unconscious instinct of the cicada. It stays underground for seventeen years and then comes forth to seek its good, which is mating. After it mates, it is satisfied. "There is Good for me," says the consciousness of the feral cats that live in the neighborhood. They find their way to the same spot each evening, awaiting the food and water that is eventually set out for them. They eat and are satisfied. They are then free to go about their business. "There is Good for me," says the nature of the seed when it is planted. As it seeks it good, it sends down rootlets and sends up a seedling. It moves toward its good and it is set free.

You can have anything you desire, provided that you are willing to pay the price for it. There is a price. And that price is to be paid with the currency of mind and spirit coins. David said, "Delight thyself also in the Lord and He shall give you the desires of your heart."[4]

There are many who would not dare teach that you can have what you want. Ernest Holmes cautions in his book, "*The Science of Mind*" that lessons on prosperity and mental control of conditions are sometimes dangerous because of the misunderstanding of this subject. This is not a "get-rich-quick" scheme; neither does it promise something for nothing.

It does, however, promise the one who will comply with its teachings that he shall be able to bring greater possibilities and happier conditions into his experience.

Ralph Waldo Emerson teaches that each of us may have whatever is truly ours. From everywhere we may take what belongs to our soul. We can't take anything else – even if all the delights of the world were within our reach. Nor can all the force of the world prevent us from receiving what is truly ours.

In seeking your good it is the "Good" that draws us to Itself. In the Bible, Jesus says, "No man can come to me, except the Father which hath sent me draw him."[5] A. W. Tozer writes *In Pursuit of God*, "That before a man can seek God; God must first have sought the man." Remember, God is Good and Good is God. An example of a toddler is one of Nature's most beautiful examples of being drawn toward your good by the "Good." Not yet able to rank or choose from the variety of experiences available to him, a toddler is led by his senses and called by every sight and sound. Given a selection of interesting shapes, colors, textures, and noisemakers, he is delighted with every new thing. He is consumed by radical involvement and play, until at night he is overpowered by fatigue and ends another day in peaceful slumber. Yet, Nature has used this radical involvement and play for her own purpose. She has worked every one of the child's abilities and encouraged his body's symmetrical growth through all the positions and movements he's gotten into trying to reach whatever has caught his attention. The child is led by natural instincts to his own good, through a process so perfect that only God could conceive it. Similarly, we are drawn to our good, by the Good, for our good. We choose what suits and delights us, and God uses our choices for our good and the good of all. God sees us in our perfection. It is all good in His eyes.

"I am seeking my Good. God is my Good." This is a simple truth that when understood and acknowledged will set me free – free from the bondages that now hold me and prevent me from my ultimate goal which is freedom and the expression of life. Jesus said, "You shall know the Truth and the truth shall make you free."[6]

Truth is changeless. It is the same yesterday, today and forever. It matters not the gender, color, country, age or religion of the messenger, the power of Truth will endure forever. Because Truth is infinite, it is continuously unfolding in our mind and in the consciousness of man. No one will ever have a *complete understanding of Truth*. A complete understanding of Truth would be a complete understanding of God, and a complete comprehension of God would be to become God. However, to the degree that you do understand and apply the truths of God, to the degree that you seek, believe and receive your Good, you are liberated. You are set free.

It is true that you CAN have what you want as long as the things that you want line up with the Will of God and do not interfere with the well-being of someone else. What is the Will of God? How will I know? We do not entirely know the Will of God. We do know that since God is the Principle and Essence of Life, the Will of God cannot be death. Therefore, we should interpret the Will of God to be everything that expresses life without hurt. Anything that will enable us to express greater life, greater happiness, greater love and greater power – so long as it does not harm anyone – must be the Will of God for us. Jesus teaches us to pray, "Thy will be done."[7] The implication relative to the "will" of God in this prayer is not a submission to the inevitability of evil or limitation; it is knowledge that the Will of God is always Good – God is Good. There is no limit to the goodness of God; therefore, there is no limit to the Good that is available for you. You mean if I want wealth, I can have it? Yes. If I want peace, I can have it? Yes. If I want happiness, I can have it? Yes. If I want to travel the world, I can do it? Yes. If I want perfect health, can I have it also? Yes, you can have it; however, know that every man must pay the price for that which he receives. It is not intended or implied that we can simply take what we wish, or that we can get something for nothing, or that it will always be done in an instant. We do not take what we wish. However, we do attract to ourselves that which is like our thought. James Allen says in his classic, *As a Man Thinketh*, "All that we achieve and all that we fail to achieve is the direct result of our own thoughts." Man must become more if he wishes to draw a greater Good into his life. There is Good for you and you ought to have it. Seek your good.

I acknowledge and believe that God is Good and Good is God. I am seeking my Good; therefore I am seeking my God. My Good is my God. As I acknowledge that the Good I am seeking must be my God, because it pulls and pushes me all the time to see if I cannot come nearer to it, I must find myself better and better satisfied. My Good draws me and causes me to move. "For in Him we live and move and have our being."[8] My Good is my God. God is my Good.

APPLYING THE PRINCIPLES

1. Every morning for the next seven days, upon awakening say, "God is Good and Good is God." Repeat, "There is Good for me and I ought to have it."

2. Make a list of the top 3 most important things that you want. Look at your list each day as you say, "There is Good for me and I ought to have it."

3. Ask yourself, "Does the most important thing that I now desire, express more life, more happiness, more peace to myself, and at the same time harms no one?" If it does, then it is right.

CHAPTER 2

Understanding the Common Good

Some of the same things that you want are the same things that other people want. There seems to be "Good" that is common to the consciousness of man. What is the common good? What is *it* that most people desire?

In an unbiased attempt to find the common good, I conducted a random survey. I asked one hundred persons the question, *"If you could have whatever you want, what would be the top three most important things that you would want?"* Every person surveyed had the opportunity to make three different responses. Ninety four (94) of the three hundred responses referred to "Wealth" as one of the first two responses. Fifty five (55) of the responses were related to "Health" as one of the first two responses. With regard to the third response, the answers varied greatly with almost as many different answers as there were persons surveyed. However, most responded with a desire that either directly or indirectly involved "Power" to control their own life or influence the lives of others.

Based upon the analysis of the survey, the common good among people is: Wealth, Health, and Power. So let us try to get a clearer understanding of each of these areas.

WEALTH

What is wealth? I think most would agree that wealth involves abundance, unlimited supply, money and prosperity. We live in a world of natural abundance. Therefore, it seems appropriate and natural that we as part of this world would want abundance or wealth. All around us there is manifested and evidence of abundance. The beaches hold countless grains of sand. A single oak tree has an abundance of leaves. The number of stars in the sky at night is untold. Who can count the number of raindrops that fall in a brief summer shower? The earth still holds a wealth of precious metals and minerals. The desire for wealth and riches is a natural and right thought for us. As Emerson once said in his *Guide to Prosperity*, "Man was born to be rich, or inevitably grows rich by the use of his faculties; by the union of thought with nature."

There is nothing wrong with wanting wealth and wanting to be rich. A desire for riches is really the desire for a richer, fuller, and more abundant life, and that desire is praiseworthy. Jesus said, "I come so that you might have life and have it more abundantly."[9] The person who does not want life more abundantly is denying his true nature and the person who does not want enough money to buy all that he desires is also denying his true nature.

If only the rich were wealthy in the way the poor fantasize. The poor admire rich people because they have a fenced in estate with carefully designed landscaping. The poor see the rich as living in large designer-furnished homes and traveling in chartered jets and limousines to distant cities and countries. Persons believing themselves to be poor, fantasize about having the time and money to travel the world or about spending as much time as they want lying on the beach of a private exotic island watching the sunsets or the sunrises. Persons believing themselves to be poor, compare what they think is the life of the "rich and famous" to their own lifestyle and feel as if they are barely surviving.

But, we don't need to live in mansions or travel in chartered jets to experience a measure of wealth. Being truly wealthy always includes experiencing the awareness of great beauty; and Nature displays great beauty for all to partake. The beauty of the sky meeting the earth is in every landscape. The stars at night glow in any backyard with the same spiritual glory that may be found in the desert of beautiful southwest Sedona. The enchanting clouds and colors of morning are available to whosoever will rise early enough to receive them. Each of us has the capacity to experience the riches that Nature offers, wherever we are. Nature's purpose is to advance and develop all of life, which means that everyone should have all that can contribute to the power, elegance, beauty, and richness of their life, and to be content with less is contrary to Nature's intent.

Although, Nature leads us on and on, somehow we never arrive. Still, we want more. The society in which we live demands that in order for us to live a really complete or successful life, in order to maximize our greatest potential, in order to develop our gifts and talents, we must use many things, and we can't have those things unless we have money to buy them with.

In seeking wealth, let us be careful not to fall prey to foolish riches. The hunger for wealth fools the eager pursuer. What is the goal of being wealthy? Surely it is to have more experiences of beauty and comfort, safe from any distressing intrusions. It is also to make life easier and to expand opportunities. The ultimate goal of wealth is to allow us the "freedom" to live life with greater satisfaction and to express life fully.

As we have already seen, the experience of beauty is easy to find. It is the repeated efforts to make life easier that often make life harder. Like most, as you acquire riches, it will be good, especially at first. It will feed the body, delight the senses, build you a mansion, afford you servants, stocks and bonds, cash, large bank accounts, real estate, designer clothes, cars, the latest and best electronics, world travel, and businesses; it will give you plenty of expensive "toys." Riches will even bring to you a multitude of friends and acquaintances. Sadly though, in the effort to acquire these things and in the pursuit to keep them, the primary purpose is too often forgotten, and the means become the end. Now, if this should happen, the wealth seeker has no room or time for truth, beauty or "Good" sense. The wealth seeker, in his fear of losing some of his wealth, becomes very stingy and unwilling to give to help his less fortunate fellow man. The unwise wealth seeker puts his quest for money above all else. He panics when he loses his smart-phone or is unable to access his e-mails or the internet. In short, it was all for nothing. You have become a slave to the ever-changing little things, the details and particulars of the day. This is the foolishness of the rich. Though we eat and drink our fill, still we hunger and thirst. We experience the literal meaning of the Buddha's First Noble Truth: "No thing ever fully satisfies."[10]

True wealth comes through understanding. Real, lasting wealth can only be acquired through understanding natural processes and working with them. It is the understanding that once you know and apply the principles and laws that govern wealth, you can do, have, and become whatever you want. True wealth comes through the understanding that when you are in union with God, that same omnipotence of God flows through you and then you know with certainty that "I can do all things." True wealth comes through the understanding that there really is no lack in your life because there is no lack in God. And God lives in you and you live, and move and have your being in God.

Once you understand the essence of the principle of wealth and apply it, once you develop a true wealth consciousness, you will attract and receive wealth. You will have the ability to set in motion and bring into manifestation – wealth. You just have to understand the right principles, apply the right law, and believe that the law will work for you.

The law is not a respecter of persons. Just like the laws of electricity or the law of gravity, it does not discriminate. Just like the laws of motion or other laws of physics, it is impersonal and neither knows nor cares who uses it, nor for what purposes. The law of wealth is compelled by its very nature to return to the user exactly what he thinks into it.

Wealth is the number one desire of most persons. If you desire wealth, then YOU can have it. You can learn how to accelerate the flow of wealth in your life. Seek your Good.

HEALTH

The second most common good that people desire is "Health." People want good health, for themselves and/or for loved ones. As with wealth, health is available and is attainable to whoever desires it. You just have to know and use the right keys that unlock the doors to health and healing; or you can even give someone else permission to do it for you.

Health is a physical, mental, as well as a spiritual state. It is the effect of the degree of harmony and balance in the total being. There are many "gifts of healing" that foster good health. I have no objection to any form of healing, for anything that helps to overcome suffering and promotes good health is good, whether it be a pill, a touch, a thought, or a prayer. Any method which produces results has its place.

The science of mind tells us that health and sickness are rooted in thought. They are effects of subjective consciousness. The subjective consciousness may be our own or the consciousness of many. It could also be the collective subjective consciousness of the entire human race as a whole. There is scientific evidence that many illnesses are the effect of our thought processes. The body will eventually respond to whatever the subjective (subconscious) mind tells it on a regular and consistent basis. The body is the servant of the mind. It obeys the operations of the mind, whether they are deliberately chosen or automatically expressed. This has been made evident in a plethora of studies on many types of various illnesses and diseases. Although, surely one does not consciously say, "Body, now I'm telling you to have high blood pressure," or "Cancer come forth," wrong thoughts and perceptions of the mind cause stress and dis-ease which manifest in the body in a number of adverse ways. Sickly thoughts will express themselves through a sickly body. Thoughts of fear have been known to kill a man as speedily as a bullet. People who live in fear of disease are often the people who get them. Anxiety quickly weakens the whole body, and lays it open to the entrance of disease; and impure thoughts, even if not physically indulged, will soon cause havoc in the nervous system. In other words, when our thinking is continuously stinking, something within is beginning to rot. Seeing that poor health and illness are rooted in thought, then to promote and encourage good health and healing we need to change and manage our thinking.

Just as wrong thoughts and negative thinking are often the underlying cause of disease and illness, strong, pure, and happy thoughts build up the body in vigor and grace. Laughter really is good medicine. The Bible gives us a perfect elixir for good health. In the Book of Philippians we are given this prescription, *"Finally, brethren, whatever things are true, whatever things are noble, whatever things are just, whatever things are pure, whatever things are lovely, whatever things are of **good report,** if there is any virtue and if there is anything praiseworthy – meditate on these things."*[11]

The body is a delicate and plastic instrument, which responds readily to the thoughts by which it is impressed, and habits of thought will produce their own effects upon it, be it good or bad.

From the standpoint of the science of mind and spirit, disease is an impersonal thing, attempting to operate and personify itself. It is a thought force, a misconception, a conviction in the mind of the one who has it, and of course, an actual experience to the one who is suffering from it. Diseases which are mental in their origin must arise from some inner state of consciousness. While most disease must first have a subjective cause, this subjective cause is not usually conscious in the thought of the person who suffers from it, but is perhaps largely the result of certain combinations of thinking. So while it is true that disease has a prototype in subjective mind, it is also true that the individual who suffers from the disease, frequently has never thought he/she was going to have that particular kind of trouble. This does not alter the fact that every disease which comes up through subjectivity, and appears in the body, must come through the mind. Even in the cases of babies or children, I feel that disease is the effect of thought that has manifested in the body as the result of combinations of collective human subconscious and wrong thought of the masses as a whole. Regardless of its particular source, disease is an experience operating through people, which does not belong to them or in them at all.

Since thought has been shown to be the underlying cause of disease and poor health, thought should be and is also the underlying cause of good health and healing. A change in diet will not benefit a man who will not change his thoughts.

According to Holmes, man is fundamentally perfect. This is the whole premise of *Science of Mind*. "Perfect God, Perfect Man, Perfect Being." Good health and healing manifest as the result of uncovering and erasing false images of thought, and embedding the truth about man's perfect being into his subjective mind. This is done through clear thinking and a systematic process of logical reasoning, which presents itself to consciousness and is acted upon by Universal Mind – God.

In presenting the truth about your own perfect being or the perfect being of someone else, you must believe, without a shadow of a doubt, that it is true. For the power of Truth alone can heal and set the captive free.

So in seeking your Good, if good health and healing is your desire, you CAN have it. You ought to have it. It is yours to receive. You can learn how to manifest healing.

POWER

The third most common good desired among people, relates directly or indirectly to "Power." People want power to have some control over their own life and/or influence the lives and behaviors of others. To have power means that you not only have the authority, but also the "dunamis" – the capability to act or cause to be.

Man perceives power through many sources. For instance, according to man, power may be held through social or economic class (the more material wealth, the more power); personal or group charisma; political process; moral persuasion (including religion); expertise (ability, skills); or force (law enforcement, military might, coercion). Of course, you and I both are familiar with the phrase "knowledge equals power." However, there is only one absolute source of power and that is the one who is "All Power" – the omnipotent God.

The more you understand and believe that you are in union with God, the more power you will be able to utilize. If God is "All Power" and God lives in you, and you live and move and have your being in God, then you have power also. "I can do all things through Christ who strengthens me." You are made in God's likeness. You have elements of the same stuff that God has. If a drop of water is taken out of the middle of the ocean, does not the drop have the same material content as the whole ocean? Does not a single cell of a body have the same DNA of that of the rest of the body? Therefore, because you are made in the image and likeness of the omnipotent God, who is "All Power," you also have power. However, just like you have to ignite a stick of dynamite to release its power, you have to ignite the power within you in order for it to work.

Faith is the catalyst that ignites power. Faith is the cause of every demonstration of power. When you have faith in something or someone, you no longer have any contradiction in your mind concerning it. You know that you know. Holmes says in *Science of Mind*, "Faith is a mental attitude which is so convinced of its own idea — which so completely accepts it — that any contradiction is unthinkable and impossible." The Bible tells us that "Now faith is the substance of things hoped for, the evidence of things not seen."[12] It is beyond the mere mumbling of words for it identifies itself with the idea (things hoped for) in such a manner that idea becomes real to the believer. The unseen becomes visible to the one with faith, and that which was untouchable becomes touchable.

Jesus said, "And these signs will follow those who believe."[13] When the realization, illumination, and revelation of your oneness with God comes upon you, when you allow the consciousness of God to dwell in you; Jesus says when the Holy Spirit has come upon you, you **shall** receive power. The Holy Spirit is the power, the "dunamis," the dynamite that dwells within you; and you activate or "stir up" the Spirit of God through faith. To those who believe, you shall receive power.

You shall receive power – to heal the sick. You shall receive power – to cast out evil. You shall receive power – to change your life and to influence the lives and behaviors of others. You shall receive power to call those things which be not as though they were – and they become. You shall receive power – to manifest wealth. You long for the day when no one will go hungry? You shall receive power to grow food in desolate places to feed the world. You long for the day when HIV and cancer is wiped off the face of the earth. You shall receive power to find a cure and educate prophylactically. You want to influence your children and family members to live a better life – you shall receive power. You want to have great impact on the world and mankind – you shall receive power. Jesus says, "With God, all things are possible."

Wealth, health and power are the common Good of most people. This is what most people want. The psalmist says, "The LORD is my Shepherd, I shall not want." And "He shall give you the desires of your heart."[14] Whatever you desire, whatever your wants are, this method that I am about to share with you when consistently applied will catapult you to receiving your Good. But, before we get into the method of making it work, it would be wise to understand self. Whether life grinds you or polishes you depends upon what you think you are made of. We can be, have, and do, all that fulfills us by following the principles and laws of mind and spirit, but for this to work, we must be who we are called to be by our true nature, our essential self. So, in the next chapter, we will take a look at the true essence of self. There is "Good" for you. You DESERVE to have it! Seek your "Good."

APPLYING THE PRINCIPLES

1. What does being wealthy mean to you? How would your life change if you were wealthy according to your definition of wealth?

2. If you could promote perfect health and healing who would it be toward? Try to see yourself or that person in perfect health, radiant with vitality and energy. How do you think it would affect your faith to be completely healed or for that person to be completely healed?

3. What does being empowered mean to you? How would your empowerment enhance your life and the lives of others?

CHAPTER 3

The True Essence of Self

MY BORN IDENTITY

Have you ever asked yourself, "Who am I? Why am I here? How did I get here? What is my purpose?" In other words, what is my "born identity?" As you evolve in self-awareness, these are the types of questions that you may ponder in your mind. I suppose that the best way to try to address these questions is to start at the beginning.

The Bible says in Genesis 1:1, "In the beginning God created . . ." Most are familiar with the well-known accounts of creation as given in the Bible and generally thought to have been recorded by Moses – ideas put into *his* thoughts of how Creation, including man, came into being. Theologians tend to think that the stories of Creation (and I said stories for there are two) are written in the Bible in the form of an allegory or symbolic story. I am not here to debate that issue today. However, I would like to share with you a brief simplified version of the creation of man from Holmes' *Science of Mind* perspective:

God (meaning the Supreme Spirit or Intelligence of the Universe) was conscious of Himself, prior to the creation of any special world system. Being thus conscious, and desiring to manifest in form, He did so manifest through the power of His Word, which is Law.

God made the mechanical universe, the plant, and animal life, but this did not satisfy Him, for He wished to create a being who could respond to and understand Him. So He created a being who had real life within himself.

He could do this only by imparting His own nature to this being whom He called man [human]. *He must make him in His own image and likeness. Man must be created out of the stuff of Eternity, if he is to have real being. Humanity must partake of the nature of Divinity if it is to have real life. So God made man* [male and female] *from the essence of Himself and clothed this subtle essence with definite form.*

And God said within Himself something after this fashion: "If I wish to have a man who is a real being, I must give him self-choice. He must be spontaneous, not automatic. He must have dominion over everything that is of less intelligence than himself. I will let him name everything I have created and he shall have all things to enjoy, for his life must be full and complete if he is to express My nature."

So God gave man dominion over all earthly things. Man was not given the power to govern the universe, but he was given the power to "have dominion." And God viewing all that He had created saw that it was good, "very good."[15]

I know that this is a rather human narrative, expressed quite differently from what you are accustomed to hearing. I hope that you are not startled by it. Just stay with me a minute and you will see how this perception of the Creation makes it a little simpler to understand your true nature.

First of all, any account of Creation implies a Universal Power, a Universal Intelligence which is omniscient – all knowing. Some may say, well what about the Big Bang theory? Even with the Big Bang theory, there had to be something, some Force, some Power, some Intelligence, some Cause that set that event (if there really was such an event, after all, it is just theory) in motion. That Universal Power, Universal Intelligence, we call God. There are many terms, outside of the religious arena, that are used to describe God. In philosophy the word *Reality* is used. Science uses the word - *Principle*. God may be termed as Spirit, Universal Mind, The Infinite, Creator, The Good, Truth, or a host of other terms. Use whatever name that feels comfortable for you – for me, I will use the name - God.

The story tells us that God created. He created the mechanical universe (the heavens and the earth, night and day; etc.) and all plant and animal life. He then created man (human) out of His own image and likeness giving him the essence of real life. Since God is Spirit, man being made in the image and likeness of God has to also be spirit. Since God is Divine, man being made in the image and likeness of God must also be divine. In order to make man a real being after His own nature, God gave man freedom of choice or free will. As human beings we were created with volition or the ability to choose for ourselves. God gave us a soul with a mind. He made man a body and then gave us dominion over all the earth. In other words, when God made man (human), He imputed to man His essence. He made man spirit, He gave man a soul or mind, and then He clothed man in definite form – He gave man a body. The premise that each human being has been created by God with three distinct entities is strengthened by our knowledge that God has three entities. God is three in one, a triune God, with three entities referred to in the Bible as the Father, the Son, and the Holy Spirit. Since God has created human beings in His image, we are led to accept that humans have been created as triune beings also, with three parts or entities that we refer to as spirit, soul and body. The Bible makes it very clear in 1st Thessalonians that we are three-part beings: "*Now may the God of peace Himself sanctify you completely; and may your whole spirit, soul, and body be preserved blameless at the coming of our Lord Jesus Christ.*"[16] Without expounding too much on theological dissertation, but, for the sake of understanding our true essence of self, let's briefly take a look at each aspect of self as made in the image of God – spirit, soul, and body.

THE SPIRIT

Jesus in talking with the woman of Samaria explained: "God is Spirit, and they that worship him must worship him in spirit and in truth."[17] Spirit is the pure essence of God. It is all of God and It is entirely apart from physical embodiment. Spirit is the All-ness of God which supports the great I AM of God. Spirit is all gender. It is male and female. It is the Father and the Mother God, because It is the Principle of Unity in all things. It is all Love, Life, Truth, Being, Power, Intelligence, Cause and Effect. It is the only Power in the universe that knows itself.

Your spirit is that part of you that is divine. It is the God in you. It is the source of power and control for your soul and body.

Your spirit is very different from your soul and body. It cannot be accessed through your five senses like your body and soul. You can feel both your body and your soul, and you are receiving information from them all the time. For example, if I asked you if you were hot or cold, you wouldn't have to pray about it and get back to me. You instantly know that. Likewise, if I asked how you felt emotionally, you don't have to study on it and tell me tomorrow. You know if you are sad or glad at any moment. It's easy to know how your body feels, what's going on in your conscious mind, and what emotions you are experiencing. However, as I mentioned your spirit is different. You simply cannot contact your spirit through your five senses or through your conscious mind, will, or emotions. In the natural, the spirit realm can't be seen or physically touched. The only way to accurately perceive spiritual truth is through the Spirit which is God. Man is *a* spirit, God is *the* Spirit. "Spirit know Thyself."

Spirit is the Power that knows Itself. Whatever that power within us is that knows itself, constitutes the part of us which is spirit or spiritual. It is the part of us that is the same essence of God. The degree apparently is different. We are like little circles within the big circle or little gods within God. Because God – Spirit, is limitless and we are in God, no limit can be placed upon the spirit of man. No limit can be placed upon you and no limit can be placed upon me.

Perhaps the one point on which all agree is that whatever the nature of Spirit, It is creative. If this were not true, nothing could have come into existence. In order to express or create, there must be a medium through which Spirit manifests, hence Soul and Body. So now let's look at the "soul" of man as created in the image of God.

THE SOUL

If you were talking to me face to face, you'd be seeing my body but speaking to my soul. The word soul is defined by some as the mind, will, and emotions and while that is certainly true, it's incomplete. The "conscious" should also be included in that definition, as well as the imagination. The soul is really what most people call the personality.

In relationship to God, I am using the word "Soul" in the sense of Universal Soul, or Medium, through which the Spirit operates. It is the Third Person of the Trinity in the Christian religion. It is the Holy Ghost. The Soul of the Universe is the Creative Medium into which the Word of God speaks and from which creation arises.

The Soul and Spirit are not entirely separate from each other. Each being Self-Existent and Co-Eternal with the other, they are really two parts or aspects of the same thing. The Soul, which is sometimes referred to as the Subjective Mind, is subjective to the Spirit. It receives impressions from the Spirit. The Soul is the doer or executor of the will of the Spirit. It is the business of the Soul to reflect the images that Spirit casts into it.

From the science of mind and spirit perspective, Soul is Subjective Intelligence, the Principle just beneath Spirit. It has the intelligence and power to produce the desire of Spirit. The Soul is the servant or executor for Spirit. Keep in mind that neither Eternal Spirit nor Eternal Soul was ever created. Each is eternal. Each is an aspect of God.

As for your personalized soul, the good news is that you can change it. Remember it is the doer or executor of the will of the spirit. You can change your soul as you change your mind. In fact, you are commanded to do so. In the book of Romans we are commanded, *"And be not conformed to this world: but be ye transformed by the renewing of your mind, that ye may prove what is that good, and acceptable, and perfect will of God."*[18] Your soul will be transformed to the degree you renew your mind, change your attitude, change your thoughts, and conform to the Word (Law) of Spirit.

Think of your soul like the valve on a faucet. It controls the rate and volume of the flow of the Spirit, God, into your body. If your mind is renewed and in agreement with the Word (Law), the valve is wide open. But, if it is in agreement with what your body is feeling or what your emotions are experiencing, or wrong thinking, then the valve is closed to the "Good" or God's life in your spirit.

Your soul – which is your mind, your emotions, your attitude, your thoughts, your consciousness, your imagination – has the power to keep every drop of your desire from ever manifesting; or it can flood your life with unlimited "Good" in every aspect of your being. If the valve is open, you will experience healing, prosperity, power, joy, victory, anointing, deliverance, and more. So, keep the valve open.

In understanding the true essence of self, lastly I want to look at the body so that we will have a picture of our "total" self.

THE BODY

Of course, your body is that physical aspect of self that you can see and touch. It is made up of the physical – the flesh, the blood, the bones, the nerves, the organs, and the cells; etc. Approximately 70% of the body is actually water. Although your body is mainly water, according to the Encyclopedia of 7700 Illustrations, if you are a healthy adult of average weight, here is what your body accomplishes in 24 hours:

Your heart beats 103,689 times.
Your blood travels 168,000,000 miles.
You breathe 23,040 times.
You inhale 438 cubic feet of air.
You eat 3 ¼ pounds of food.
You drink 2.9 quarts of liquids.
You lose 7/8 pound of waste.
You speak 4,800 words.
You move 750 muscles.
Your nails grow .000046 inch.
Your hair grows .01714 inch.
You exercise 7,000,000 brain cells.

The body's entire structure from head to foot is an instrument of precision engineering and production. The psalmist says in Psalm 139, "I praise you, for I am fearfully and wonderfully made."[19]

In the Science of Mind, the word "body" means the entire manifestation of Spirit on all planes. Body is the result of Spirit working through Soul. The entire manifestation of Spirit, both visible and invisible, is the Body of God. The physical universe is the Body of God.

Our physical being is the body of our unseen man. Our soul and spirit permeates our body. Traditionally, we have heard that our body is the temple or dwelling place of our soul — our consciousness. According to Holmes, we would not say that consciousness is in the body, but rather the *body is in consciousness*!

The physical body is for the purpose of allowing consciousness to function on this plane. The body is necessary to this plane, since only through a physical body can we physically function here. When the body is no longer a fit instrument to allow the soul to operate on this plane, the soul deserts it and continues to function on another plane. I believe that is what Paul meant when he said in 2nd Corinthians 5:8, "To be absent from the body is to be present with the Lord."

The body and the condition of the body is always an effect, never a cause. Effect is that which did not make itself, but must have a power backing it, causing it to be. All manifestation, all form, all body, including our physical flesh and blood body is effect, and is subject to its cause.

The body itself is not intelligent and does not have volition or free-will. However, it does express the intelligence of the soul or consciousness. The consciousness (soul) so completely engulfs the body that the body appears to have an intelligence of its own. Some say that the mind completely controls the body, and that the body is but a reflection of the mind. In no way am I trying to contradict the reality of the body or bodily experiences; however, I am trying to point out that your body is an instrument or machinery, permeated and used by your consciousness (soul) to carry out the will of the Spirit. Good health, poor health, disease, and pain are all effects that manifest in the body as a result of subjective mind.

Psychology has proven that disturbances in the mind produce physical reactions in the body. So, if you want your body to be well and in good health, then your soul or subjective mind must be poised and peaceful. As a general rule, when all is well in your soul, all will be well with your body. As the Bible writer says, "Beloved, I pray that you will prosper and be in good health, even as your soul prospers."[20]

So there you have it, the essence of your true self – Spirit, Soul and Body. Each part is vital and indispensable to be whole and complete. Although brief, this should help clarify who you really are.

So far, we have identified the "Good." You have named your good. We have looked at the common good, and have glanced at our true essence of self. You are almost ready to proceed through the process, to engage the method that will catapult you into manifesting your desire.

The process of manifesting your desire and experiencing your "good" involves applying proven universal principles and laws of the science of mind and spirit. In metaphysics, which simply means that which is above and beyond the physical, there are natural laws and principles that work, just like there are natural laws and principles that work in the physical world. For instance, the laws of electricity, the law of gravity, and the laws of motion are all laws of physics – the physical. The law of attraction, the law of gratitude, and the law of giving, are universal laws of mind and spirit that have been proven to work each and every time that they are applied; just as with the physical laws.

It will not be necessary for you to study in depth any of the principles or laws in order for them to work for you. As with any law of nature, it is not a respecter of persons and does not care who uses it. All you have to do is apply it and *know* that it will work. When you turn on your light switch you may not know why the light comes on but you do know and expect that with a light bulb that is good, the light will come on. The same is with any physical or metaphysical law. You do not have to be an expert as to the why, all you have to do is *know* that it will. However, because it may prove helpful to your faith in believing that the process will work for you, in the next chapter I will give you a brief overview of this science, and each of the principles and laws that we will be using in the process for you to experience and receive your "Good." There is "Good" for you. And you CAN have it!

APPLYING THE PRINCIPLES

You are a triune being – spirit, soul, and body. Your spirit is different from your soul and body in that it cannot be accessed through your five senses. Your spirit is that part of you that is divine. Centering prayer is a good meditative practice to experience the gift of Divine Presence and Unity. It is a silent, meditation of simply resting in Universal Oneness, which is God. It involves participation and cooperation of the total you – spirit, soul, and body. Practice the following exercise for 20 minutes once a day.

1. First choose a sacred word that best supports your intention to be in God's presence and open to His divine action within you ("Jesus", "God", "Abba", "Divine", "Spirit", "Father" etc.).

2. Now sit comfortably, close your eyes, relax and quiet your mind and body.

3. Gently release all cares, concerns, feelings, and images. Allow your soul and your body to peacefully rest in the silence and stillness.

4. Whenever you become aware of anything (thoughts, feelings, images, perceptions, etc.) simply whisper your sacred word and return to the silence.

CHAPTER 4

The Principles and Laws of this Science

WHAT IS THIS SCIENCE

Science in general is the knowledge of facts based upon some proven principle. The scientific investigation of anything is, of necessity, a matter-of-fact, emotionless proposition. We speak about science being an absolute knowledge. Science is absolute knowledge as long as it is demonstrable and repeatable. There are many sciences. This science that we will use to accelerate manifestation of your "Good" is the science of mind and spirit. The science of mind and spirit is the study of Life and the nature of the laws of thought; the concept that we live in a spiritual Universe; and that God is in, through, around, and for us. It is based upon proven principles that Good is Universal, and that as much good as any individual is able to incorporate into his life is his or hers to use.

There is nothing supernatural anywhere, on any plane. That which today seems to us to be supernatural, after it is understood and its principles have been repeatedly demonstrated, we will find it to be spontaneously natural.

In the scientific discovery of laws, certain theories are postulated. This may happen through research and investigation. When the theory proves to be correct, after many experiments, then a principle is announced. In this way scientific truth is demonstrated. The principle of any science is invisible, theoretical, as in our idea of Spirit. No one has seen God. No one has seen Life; we see the manifestation of Life.

The sciences are objectively real to us only in so far as the principles can be demonstrated. Until we can demonstrate the principles, it is only suppositional as far as practical results are concerned. As a matter of fact, we really only know as much as we can prove by actual demonstration.

As soon as a law is discovered, experiments are made with it. Certain facts are proven to be true and in this way a science is gradually formulated. Any science consists of a number of known facts about its invisible principle. As more and more facts are gathered and proven, the science expands and gradually becomes accepted and may be used by anyone, whether they understand it or not.

The science of mind and advances in the laws of thought are now beginning to be used in leading institutions of medicine and business. These are the same principles that have been used by metaphysicians and New Thought thinkers since long ago, including Plato, Socrates, and Aristotle. However, the world at large has not yet come to consider the principles of mental practice in the same light that it considers other more traditional principles of life and action. This is primarily due to the fact that the principles of metaphysics seem less tangible to the average person than other principles; plus, they are misunderstood based on the lack of proper teaching and training. In order for most people to believe a principle and accept it as a law or truth of nature, they need to see concrete demonstration with positive results. We tend to talk about the power of mind and thought much more than we demonstrate its efficacy.

It is of paramount importance that we practice what we preach. We have to demonstrate, not only for our personal benefit, but for the benefit of all, that this science and these principles really do and will work. In using this science, many methods have been formulated that will produce results. Some involve years of study and practice of metaphysics. The truth has many ways in which it can be expressed. And as this science is more widely studied and practiced, I feel certain that more truths in this area will be discovered.

This guidebook, however, is intended for persons, like you and I, whose most pressing need is to see results in getting their "Good" especially in the areas of wealth, health, and power. It is for those who have, so far, not found the time, the means, or the opportunity to plunge deeply into the study of metaphysics; but who want results and who are willing to take the conclusions of science as a basis for action, without delving into all the processes by which those conclusions were reached. It is expected that you will take the fundamental statements on faith, just as you would take statements concerning laws of motion as they were promulgated by Newton; and taking the statements on faith, that you will prove their truth by acting upon them without fear or hesitation. However, if you wish to investigate philosophical theories and so secure a logical basis for faith, I will now give you a brief overview of eight fundamental principles and universal laws that you will be applying as you follow the method that will accelerate the manifestation of your "good."

THE LAW OF DIVINE UNITY

This law states that all life, all energy, all consciousness are connected and that we are one. We all come from the same source and are all living expressions of the Divine. We are all connected. We are in God and God is in us. Our true essence is spiritual consciousness. This is where all potentiality and creativity can be found. Knowing your true self is knowing that you have ability to fulfill any desire or dream that you have because you are one with the One that is the Creator of all things that ever were, are, or ever will be. You are that "Good" that you seek. Speak only truth about yourself.

THE LAW OF CAUSE AND EFFECT

This Law is also known as the Iron Law of Human Destiny because it is so profound and powerful. Simply stated, the Law of Cause and Effect says that everything happens for a reason. All actions have consequences, as do all inactions. Distilled down to the simplest possible terms, this law states that every effect in one's life is the result of a specific cause which is rooted in thought.

The truly wonderful thing about this law is that by definition then, we should be able to manifest that which we want (the effect) simply by exerting specific thought (cause).

THE LAW OF ATTRACTION

The Law of Attraction states that we attract into our lives that which we focus our thoughts upon. If your thoughts are constantly on positive outcomes and good results, then that is what you will manifest. If, on the other hand your predominant thoughts are on negative outcomes and poor results, then that is what you will attract. This is based on the fact that the Universe is simply vibrational energy in motion. Emotions, thoughts, feelings and objects – absolutely everything has a vibrational frequency. Since with vibration, like attracts like, it is logical that the vibrational frequency of your predominant thoughts will attract results that have a similar vibrational frequency.

We can use the Law of Attraction to attract what we want because we have free-will to choose our predominant thought.

THE LAW OF GIVING

The Law of Giving or the Law of Divine Reciprocity is a universal law that says, "Give and you shall receive." You give and God gives in return. This Law can also be called the Law of Giving and Receiving because the universe operates through dynamic exchange. Every relationship within the universe is one of giving and receiving. Giving engenders receiving, and receiving engenders giving. In reality, receiving is the same thing as giving, because giving and receiving are different aspects of the flow of energy in the universe. And if you stop the flow of either, you interfere with nature's intelligence.

The more you give, the more you will receive, because you will keep the abundance of the universe circulating in your life. In fact, anything that is of value in life only multiplies when it is given. If through the act of giving, you feel that you have lost something, then the gift is not truly given and will not cause increase. If you give grudgingly there is no energy behind that giving.

The intention behind your giving and receiving should always be to create happiness for yourself and the receiver, because happiness is life-supporting and life-sustaining and therefore generates increase. Your return is directly proportional to your giving when you give unconditionally and from the heart.

THE LAW OF COMPENSATION

The Law of Compensation is another restatement of the Law of Sowing and Reaping. It says you will always be compensated for your efforts and for your contribution, whatever it is, however much or however little. In other words, every act rewards itself. Ralph Waldo Emerson, in his essay, "Compensation," wrote that each person is compensated in like manner for that which he or she has contributed. Jesus said, "For with the same measure that you use, it will be measured back to you."[21]

Your mental attitude, your feelings of happiness and satisfaction, are the result of the things that you have put into your own mind. If you fill your mind with thoughts, visions and ideas of success, happiness and optimism, you will be compensated by those positive experiences in your daily activities. Likewise, the income you earn today is your compensation for what you have done in the past. If you want to increase your compensation, you must increase the value of your contribution.

THE LAW OF EXPECTATION

Simply stated, the Law of Expectation tells us that whatever you expect, with confidence, whether positive or negative becomes self-fulfilling. Researchers in Britain and Germany wrote an important article on the Law of Expectation published in the Science Translational Journal. They used brain imaging (MRI) to show "expectations can cancel out the benefits of Pain Killing drugs." Viewing the brain scans, the researchers discovered that the brain's pain networks responded to different degrees based on the patient's amount of "expectation" of a successful treatment. According to the lead author, Irene Tracy of Oxford University, "The brain imaging is telling us that patients really are switching on-and-off parts of their brains – through the mechanism of Expectation."[22]

Pharmaceutical companies found this research very important. Why? If patients can destroy the power of the drugs they take by their "expectations," clinical trials had to be changed to overcome this problem because the U.S. Food and Drug Administration could reject their application to offer certain drugs for sale in the United States. Each drug must pass tests to prove it is more effective than a mere sugar pill or placebo. No scientific proof, no stamp of approval.

Today there is absolute valid scientific evidence to prove that our feelings and past experiences can influence, persuade and convince our mind-body-connection to cause positive or negative results by the power of our brain to 'expect' good or bad conclusions.

When you expect with confidence that good things will happen, they usually do. If you confidently expect to succeed, if you confidently expect to be healed, if you confidently expect to be wealthy as a result of applying your talent and abilities to your opportunities and you maintain that attitude of confident expectation long enough, it will become your reality. We will work harder and longer to get what we want, if we "expect" the results to be what we choose. The Law of Expectation changes the odds in our favor to win because our brain motivates us to do whatever it takes to reach our goal. Whatever is the "Good" that you seek, "expect" to receive it and you will have it.

THE LAW OF FAITH

The Law of Faith is simple. It means that whatever you believe wholeheartedly without any doubt, fear, or contradiction, will come to pass. Faith is a proven universal law which when operated properly works every time without fail. A plethora of scientific research studies have been completed and support the power of "faith"; especially in the area of healing. Just like the Laws of aerodynamics, or the Laws of electromagnetism, or any natural law, faith works consistently for anyone and everyone who uses it. The Bible says, "Whatsoever things ye desire, when ye pray, believe that ye receive them and ye shall have them." Notice that there is no limitation, "Whatsoever things" is very definite and implies that the only limitation which is placed upon us is our ability to think. Remember that faith is not a shadow, but a substance, "the substance of things hoped for, the evidence of things not seen." By using the law of faith you can obtain anything you want; you can have your "good."

The degree to which you believe is directly proportional to how quickly and how solid your "good" will manifest. Many people experience faith in varying amounts at different times and with different results. This is because their measure of faith fluctuates. Faith is not an immeasurable thing because the Bible says God has dealt to every man the measure of faith. Therefore, faith can be measured and can be increased or decreased. The greater the faith you have, the greater the manifestation. "According to your faith, let it be to you."

THE LAW OF GRATITUDE

The Law of Gratitude is based on the natural principle that action and reaction are always equal and in opposite directions. Sir Isaac Newton applied this long-known metaphysical principle to physical objects in the 1600's when he formulated his law of motion saying, "For every action, there is an equal and opposite reaction" (Newton's Third Law). This means that an action leading outward is always accompanied by a reaction coming inward. So the action of expressing thankful praise to the Creator always solicits a reaction toward us. Our gratitude liberates an energy within us that immediately expands into the Omnipotent, where it is instantly returned to us in kind. If your gratitude is strong and constant, the response of the Creator will be strong and continuous, and the things you want will always move toward you. Notice the grateful attitude Jesus maintained, how he always seemed to be saying, "I thank you, Father, that you have heard me." You can't exercise much power without gratitude, for gratitude is what keeps you connected with Power. Give thanks for your "Good" as it moves toward you.

These are the proven Universal Laws and Principles that you will employ as you follow the method in the next chapter that will accelerate the manifestation of your "Good." There is one more Universal Law that is the greatest of all, which encompasses all of the laws of this science. And that is the Law of Love.

THE LAW OF LOVE

"Though I speak with the tongues of men and of angels, but have not love, I have become sounding brass or a clanging cymbal."[23]

The Law of Love says to first love God with all your heart, soul and mind; and second, to love your neighbor as you love yourself. The greater this virtue called love is expressed, the greater the bond of divine unity which opens the door making all things possible. Love is the essence, the glue and the fabric of all that is and is the energy that moves through all. It is the greatest of all the Laws. Every religion teaches the Law of Love:

Buddhism — *Hurt not others with that which pains yourself.* Udanavarga 5.18.

Christianity — *Whatever you want men to do to you, do also to them, for this is the Law and the Prophets.* Matthew 7:12.

Hinduism — *This is the sum of duty: Do nothing to others which if done to you, would cause you pain.* Mahabharata 5.1517.

Islam — *No one of you is a believer until he loves for his brother what he loves for himself.* Traditions.

Jainism — *In happiness and suffering, in joy and grief, we should regard all creatures as we regard our own self, and should therefore refrain from inflicting upon others such injury as would appear*

undesirable to us if inflicted upon ourselves.
Yogashastra 2.20.

Judaism —   *What is hurtful to yourself do not to your*
fellow man. That is the whole of The Torah and
the remainder is but commentary. Go learn it.
Talmud.

Sikhism —   *As you deem yourself so deem others. Then you will*
become a partner in partner to heaven. Kabir.

Taoism —   *Regard your neighbor's loss as your own loss.* T'ai
shang kan ying p'ien.

If you truly want to accelerate the manifestation of your "Good" then let everything that you do be done out of love, in love and through love. Remember, God — Universal Consciousness, Creator, Spirit, the Omnipotent One, is Love. So when you operate through Love you are operating through All Power, through God, and nothing is impossible for you.

In the next chapter, I will give you the method that if you follow it without reservation, hesitation, or alteration, it will catapult you into a new realm and the desires that were once merely dreams WILL become your reality. Will it be easy? That's left up to you. Any mental or spiritual evolution requires discipline and training. There is a price to be paid. You will have to overcome distractions both physical and mental. You will have to tune out the naysayers. You will have to discipline yourself to stick with it. And there are sacrifices to be made (you may have to give up some TV time or wake up a little bit earlier). In the beginning it may appear to you that nothing is happening. Know for certain that something is happening. Your desire is in the process of manifesting. Do not stop. Do not give up. Be dedicated and determined. There is "good" for you and you are receiving. I once watched the process of a huge convention center being constructed in downtown Nashville. I passed the site weekly on my way to work. For approximately two and a half years, I could see no evidence of any construction. All the work was being done deep in the ground. There was a safety fence around the site which prevented me from even seeing the bulldozers that were daily preparing the foundation for the great structure that would soon be erected. I passed that site weekly with only the thought and the assurance that I heard from others that a new convention center was being built. Then one day, as I was approaching the site, I notice construction above ground in plain sight. It seemed to have appeared overnight. After that, the remainder of the construction of that massive convention center seemed to have been accelerated. The physical, visual, above-ground fruition of that great edifice took much less time than the planning stage and laying the foundation for manifestation. I found out later that just the planning of that project had been in the making for over ten years. Similarly, such will be with the manifestation of your good. When you think nothing is happening, change you thought and know for certain that something is happening and soon you will see it. It all involves transforming and renewing your thought process using Universal Laws that have been scientifically proven to work. All the essential work is done in your mind.

This process has been organized and developed into an easy to follow step-by-step method for your success. Know for certain that you, like many others, can do this. YOU CAN follow this method that I'm about to share with you and in doing so your life will change in ways you cannot imagine. You will soon begin to think differently and in thinking differently you will become different and what you have will be different. Say to yourself right now, "There is Good for me and I ought to have it." Will it be worth it? You bet! "Eye have not seen, nor ear heard, nor have entered into the heart of man the things which God has prepared for those who love Him." Success is in your hands (rather, in your thoughts would be more accurate). There is Good for you and you can have it. This science will work for you. This method will work for you if you are willing to follow it. Let's now begin and prove that it works.

APPLYING THE PRINCIPLES

1. The Law of Love is the greatest of all the spiritual laws. How would you define love? What could you do to express more love to your neighbor, your family, and to yourself?

2. For the next seven days, practice leaving a gift with everyone you meet. It could be a silent gift such as a smile, a good thought or a silent prayer. It could be a spoken gift such as a compliment or a greeting; or it could be a material gift – monetary or non-monetary. Make a note of all gifts, regardless of how big or small, that Nature gives to you during this period as you give to others.

3. Practice the Law of Expectation at elevators. When you have a choice of multiple elevators, stand in front of the one that you "expect" to open. As you do this repeatedly, notice how the elevator that you "expect" to open does so more frequently than the others. You can also do similar exercises when looking for parking spaces.

---- CHAPTER 5 ----

The Accelerated Method

This method to accelerate the manifestation of your "good" involves a seven-step process. You should diligently apply and concentrate on one step per week. In order for this system to work for you, you must be dedicated and determined to go through the complete process. Many read books, take home study courses and attend lectures all their lives without ever making any progress in demonstrating the value of the principles involved because they do not apply the method. Apply this method and prove to yourself and others that these laws and principles really do work. Do not be tempted to work ahead. Do not skip steps. Each step should be followed exactly as it is presented. Each step builds upon the previous step. The steps within themselves have valid reliability and will produce results independently; however, it is this complete method that will *accelerate* the time and solidity of the manifestation of your desire. Some assignments are repeated. This is intentional. You will need a small journal or notebook that will be easy to carry around with you. Remember to follow the method as it is presented. Do this complete method as many times as necessary until your desire manifests. The more you do it, the more effective you will become. And as you repeatedly practice this method, you will evolve in Divine Consciousness and nothing will be impossible for you. There is Good for you and you ought to have it. If you truly want what is rightfully yours, if you are ready to start receiving, if you are ready for change, then let's get started with the first step.

STEP 1
This first step is designed to get a clear concise understanding of what you want. So be as specific as possible. First, name specifically what you want. This is your "good." Why do you want it? Ask yourself, "Does this thing that I want express more life, more happiness, and more freedom for me and at the same time harm no one?" If the answer is yes, then it is right for you. Say to yourself throughout the day specifically what you want. Write down in your journal what you want – your "good." Be specific. If you could see it, how would it look? What color is it? Does it have shape? If you could touch it, how would it feel? If you could hear it, how would it sound? If you could smell it, how would it smell? When would you like to have it? Write down a date. Answer this question, "If I receive my _____ on today what would I do, how would I feel?" Will others also benefit from you having it or just you? Think about the answer. Write it down in your journal.

Describe your perfect day after having received your desire. Write it in your journal.

For the next seven days continue to fine tune and add to this journal entry identifying your desire.

Read what you wrote at least 2 times each day. Read it out loud to yourself before going to bed and early each morning. Each time that you read it, thank God for your "good" (say the name of it).

Dear God,

I thank You for my _____. *I am receiving. Right now, I am receiving.*

Do this for seven days, then move on to Step 2.

STEP 2

Step 2 is to allow time for Divine union and communication through meditation. This practice is vital for spiritual empowerment. The exercise involves simply sitting in silence for 20 minutes. Choose a time that you can easily stick to. The evening works best for me. You may choose to wake up early before daybreak when everything is quiet and still. Your mind is usually more at peace during this time of morning. Choose a comfortable chair. Sit erect. Close your eyes (but, don't go back to sleep). Then be still and inhibit all thoughts. This may be difficult at first. You may find that a great number of thoughts are constantly trying to gain access to your mental world. You can use a word – a one or two syllable positive word, to center yourself back to silence when you find that thoughts begin to flood your mind. If thoughts begin to bombard your mind say the word softly to yourself and just let the thoughts pass. Do not focus on the thoughts. Say the word as often as you need for the thoughts to pass. Also, do not focus on the word. You want to just relax your body, inhibit all thought and partake of the silence. With practice you will be able to control your thoughts at will. After meditating in silence for about 20 minutes, thank God that you are receiving your good – your desire. REPEAT: *"God I thank you that we are one. You are in me and I am in You. I thank You for my _____. I am receiving. Right now, I am receiving."*

If you do your meditation early in the mornings, read your journal afterwards. Re-read your journal before going to bed. Do this exercise for seven days, then move on to Step 3.

STEP 3
Step 3 will help you acknowledge the truth about yourself. Regardless of outward appearance, you must only speak the truth concerning yourself. Most of us forget what we look like as soon as we step away from the mirror. Thus, we find it difficult to truly picture ourselves. Do this exercise standing in front of the mirror. Look yourself in the eyes as you declare the following truths concerning yourself. Allow yourself approximately five minutes of uninterrupted time to do this. If privacy is an issue, go in the bathroom and lock the door. Stand in front of the mirror. Be sure to *look yourself in the eyes* as you say:

I am made in the image and likeness of God. I am perfect for God is perfect. God lives in me, God lives through me, and God is for me. I live and move and have my being in God. I am in God and I am of God. We are one. I am receiving what I desire for there is no want in

God and God is in me. There is no lack in my life for there is no lack in God. God is in me and I am in God and I am of God. We are one. I am wealthy for God is wealth and God is in me and I am in God. There is no illness, there is no disease, there is no pain in my life for there is no illness, there is no disease, there is no pain in God and we are one. I radiate divine health for God is health and God is in me and I am in God. There is no weakness, there is no fear in my life for there is no weakness, there is no fear in God. We are one. I am one with the Omnipotent, Omniscient, Omnipresent Good. God lives in me and is for me. Everything works for my good. The great I AM works inevitably in me and through me to will and to do that which ought to be done by me. I am receiving my good. God is my good. I am receiving my desire. Right now, I am receiving my _____ *. God I thank You. I am receiving.* REPEAT

A good time to do this step is when you are alone in the bathroom, preferably following your meditation if you meditate in the morning. Continue to re-read your journal entry during the morning and before going to sleep at night. Do this exercise every morning for seven days, then move on to Step 4.

STEP 4

Step 4 is designed to use conscious thought to impress upon Universal Mind by way of subjective thought. In this step you will affirm and concentrate your thought upon your ideal — your good, as an already existing fact. Thought concentrated on a definite purpose becomes power. Through repeated conscious affirmations of already having, being, or doing what you desire, you will set in motion the creative response of your subjective thought which impresses upon Universal Mind and causes manifestation to happen. Your desire becomes your reality. Do not concern yourself as to how it will manifest. Just know that the process is underway and manifestation will come to fruition. Since your "good" is individualized and personalized, I will give you a general affirmation based on the common good of most people. You can individualize it by filling in the blanks with your personal desire. REPEAT:

There is Good for me and I am receiving. My Good that I am receiving is my _____. I am/have _____. My _____ that I am receiving is mine to have. I am/have _____. My _____ that I am receiving, I ought to have. It is mine. My _____ is flowing to me right now. I am a _____ magnet. I am attracting everything I need for my _____ to manifest. My _____ comes to me quickly, effortlessly, and continuously. I am receiving. Right now, I am receiving my _____. And God I give you thanks. I thank you dear God for my _____. I am/ have _____.

Say this affirmation each morning after you repeat the "truths" concerning yourself while looking in the mirror. Say it again each night after you read your journal entry. Do this for seven days and then move on to Step 5.

STEP 5

In Step 5 you will give more fuel to your affirmation by "revving it up" with visualization. To visualize means mentally seeing the things that you wish to have or to do. When you mentally see the things you desire, and see them clearly, you are presenting Universal Mind with images of thought; and It at once tends to project them into form. The form will depend upon the mental images from which it emanates. This will depend upon the depth of the impression, the predominance of the idea, the clarity of the vision, and the boldness of the image. If the thought image is clear, it provides a good mold. If it is imperfect the mold is a poor one. This does not mean that you must set your mind or hold thoughts. It simply means that you must think clearly. A good time to do this exercise is at night before going to sleep. First, re-read your journal entry. Next repeat your affirmation. Then, as you relax your body, settling down for sleep, visualize yourself as having your desire. See the complete outcome of your desire in mental pictures in every detail. See yourself interacting as the leading character. As you close your eyes continue to envision in your mind clear details of having your desire as you enter into sleep. Do this exercise for seven nights before moving on to Step 6.

STEP 6

Step 6 involves an exercise that will keep the act of receiving continuously flowing to you. It consists of the Law of Giving. Practicing the Law of Giving will keep the abundance of the Universe circulating in your life. The more you give, the more you shall receive. In fact, anything that is of value in life only multiplies when it is given. The return is directly proportional to the giving when it is unconditional and from the heart. The measure in which you give is the measure in which you will receive. In other words, if you want love then give love. If you want joy, learn to give joy. If you want to be materially affluent, help others to become materially affluent. The easiest way for you to get what you want is to help others get what they want. If you want to be blessed with all the good things in life, learn to silently bless everyone with all the good things in life. The best way to start the whole process of circulation is to make a decision that anytime you come in contact with anyone you will give them something. It doesn't have to be in the form of something material. It can be a smile, a good thought, a silent prayer, a greeting or a compliment. It can even be an act of caring, attention, appreciation, affection or an act of love. These are some of the most precious gifts and they do not cost you anything.

To apply Step 6, make a decision to give to whomever you encounter, wherever you go. Give cheerfully and willingly. As long as you are giving, you will be receiving. Receive gratefully all the gifts that life has to give you. Make note in your journal of all the gifts that start to come your way as you start to give. It may be a good parking space, an exceptionally beautiful sunset or even unexpected money. Do this exercise for the next seven days as you continue to practice the previous steps. Then move on to the final step of this method.

STEP 7

Step 7 involves exercising your belief – your faith. You now have everything that you need to enhance your life and have what you want. The one thing left in this process that will accelerate the manifestation of your desire is your faith. Your faith can slow down the process or catapult you through the process of manifestation; however, it cannot prevent the laws from working. The laws will work regardless. Your faith determines the acceleration and speed of completion of manifestation. The more you believe and know that these principles and laws will work for you, the sooner you will have your "good." You must BELIEVE, KNOW AND EXPECT that this method of application will work for you. You must be dedicated and dependable in applying this method in order to be "transformed by the renewing of your mind." BELIEVE, KNOW AND EXPECT that you are one with God. BELIEVE, KNOW AND EXPECT that God lives in you, through you, and is for you. BELIEVE, KNOW AND EXPECT that you live and move and have your being in God. Because you are one with God, nothing is impossible for you; for nothing is impossible for God. BELIEVE, KNOW AND EXPECT that there is Good for you and you ought to have it. BELIEVE, KNOW AND EXPECT that you can have what you want. BELIEVE, KNOW AND EXPECT that if you have followed this method that you WILL have what you want. BELIEVE, KNOW AND EXPECT that there are Universal Laws that are working for you right now. Your desire IS manifesting. BELIEVE, KNOW AND EXPECT that regardless and irrespective of any false appearance that nothing is happening, if you have followed this method, something is happening. Your "good" is manifesting and will come into fruition. Get excited! Be thankful! Expect it! YOU WILL HAVE WHAT YOU WANT! "According to thy faith, be it unto thee."

APPLYING THE PRINCIPLES

In summary, *The Accelerated Method* to get what you want involves the following seven steps:

Step 1:   Identify in writing what you want.

Step 2:   Meditate in silence for 20 minutes each day.

Step 3: Speak "Truth" about your unity with God.
Step 4: Affirm your being/having what you want in present tense.
Step 5: Visualize your being/having what you want in detail.
Step 6: Learn to cheerfully give in like measure.
Step 7: Believe it. Know it. Expect it.

Apply each step for seven days before moving on to the next step. Complete the entire method. Remember it is the application of this complete method that will cause the accelerated manifestation of your desire. Be determined to get what you want. Apply this method and watch the results.

CHAPTER 6

The Results

If you have been diligent in following this method, the fruit of your labor – your "Good" – will soon be realized if it has not already manifested. You have, thus far, invested approximately one hour each day for about forty nine days to enhance and change your life forever. If necessary repeat the method. Do it again. Continue to practice these exercises every day until you see results. YOU WILL RECEIVE WHAT YOU WANT. This is a science. Its principles and laws have been repeatedly proven, demonstrated and will work for anyone and everyone who applies them, including you!

As with any new skill, discipline or thought process, the more you practice the better you will become in applying the principles. The better you become, the stronger your faith and confidence become. The stronger your faith becomes the sooner your desire will manifest. You can learn to master this method to demonstrate universal laws in such a way that nothing will be impossible for you. Already your thoughts have changed in such a way as to set things in motion for your desire to manifest. Keep in mind, there are no coincidences. The circumstances and favor that now comes your way are effects of your thoughts that you have developed while following this method. You will find that you will meet just the right people. Some persons that are a hindrance to your success may drop out of your life. Opportunities will come your way. Prosperous ideas may seem to come out of nowhere. Your health is improving. You influence people more readily. You have greater joy. You seem to be what one may call "lucky." You are being transformed by the renewing of your mind. The "good" that you desire will come to you easily, effortlessly and continuously. As a matter of fact, although you initially set out to acquire something that you desired, something that you wanted, in the process, as you have applied this method of science a change has automatically happened within you. Your thinking has changed. You have evolved.

OLD THINGS HAVE PASSED AWAY; ALL THINGS HAVE BECOME NEW

Thinking is the only activity which the spirit possesses, and thought is the only product of thinking. Every thought brings into action physiological tissue, parts of the brain, nerve or muscle. This produces an actual physical change in the conformation of the tissue. Therefore, it is only necessary to have a certain number of thoughts on a given subject in order to bring about a complete change in your physical organization, a new you. This method in which you have followed encourages and facilitates right thinking. New thoughts of courage, power, inspiration, divine unity, harmony, and success are substituted for old thoughts of failure, despair, lack, limitation, and discord; and as these new thoughts take root, the physical tissue is changed. You will find that persons will begin to tell you that there is something different about you. You see life in a new light. Old things have passed away, all things have become new. You are born again, this time born of the spirit. Life has new meaning for you. You are reconstructed and are filled with joy, confidence, hope, energy. You see opportunities for success to which you were before blind. You recognize possibilities which before had no meaning for you. The thoughts of success and having what you want, with which you have been impregnated, are radiated to those around you, and they in turn help you onward and upward. You attract to yourself new circumstances, new friends and associates, and this in turn changes your environment. This is the process by which failure is changed to success. This is the process by which the substance of things hoped for become evident and are seen. By using this method of new thought we can literally change our world through an exponential shift.

CHAPTER 7

An Exponential Shift

Imagine living in a world where poverty is rarely heard of. Everyone has access to what they need and want without trying to take from someone else. Imagine a world that when someone is sick instead of going to the hospital or scheduling a physical examination, they get a check-up from the neck up. Their thinking is examined. Right thought is then prescribed for cure. Imagine cancer, HIV, diabetes, heart disease, Alzheimer's, all gone. Imagine a world where hunger is eradicated. No more pictures of starving children. No more cruelty to innocent animals. A world of peace and love. A world where persons are no longer judged by their bank accounts or the color of their skin; but, rather by the content of their hearts and thoughts. Imagine watching the evening news and only good is being reported; criminal and civil offenses alike, being seldom committed. War and bloodshed for boundaries and control are no longer practiced. Imagine being able to redirect the path of a hurricane or commanding the wind of a tornado to be still and it obeys. Do you think this can never be? Sounds impossible?

Less than two hundred years ago, it sounded impossible that man would ever be able to light up his home merely by flipping a switch. Less than one hundred years ago few would have believed that man would someday be able to sit in a room in Akron, Ohio or Chattanooga, Tennessee and watch a live football game taking place in Seattle, Washington. Or that man would be able to travel to the other side of the world in less than a day. Less than fifty years ago who would have ever thought that the use of a cellular phone less than the size of a playing card would be our most common means of communication; or that computers would be an everyday household commodity. Less than ten years ago mainstream science would not have believed that an amputee would be able to functionally operate and use his prosthetic arm with just the power of his thought.

You will see, you must see, that we are at the dawn of a new day; that the possibilities are so wonderful, so fascinating, so limitless as to be almost bewildering. Any person with knowledge of the possibilities contained in the principles of this method that you have been given has an inconceivable advantage over the multitudes.

However, this knowledge is not just for you and me. It is to be shared. It is to be proclaimed. You must tell somebody. While applying this method for the sake of your body, your business, or intellect, your thoughts for the time being would be like shells filled only with desire. As you continue to evolve and mature in these laws and principles you will strike a moment when you will realize and see that this science is to be practiced for its own sake. This science is not a new enterprise by which to make money, nor a new patented medicine, nor a new chemical for increasing brain forces. It is for freedom and the expression of the soul. It is for all who will embrace it. It is "Truth" that will set men free.

Jesus tells us to go into all the world and spread the good news – "The Kingdom of God is at Hand."[24] There are many others like yourself who are seeking their "good." There are many who are in bondage and seek to be free. Now that you know the way, you must help your fellow brother or sister. You must tell someone of these "Truths." If you tell someone, and then they tell someone and so on and so on; if enough of us who have discovered these "Truths" will go into all the world and proclaim this "Good News"; if enough of us will do this, then sooner or later there will be enough like-mindedness to cause a global shift in human consciousness and our world will truly be as one – united through One Mind, united through thought, and united through the "Good."

There is good for you. There is good for me. There is good for all and as much good as you can incorporate into your life is just waiting to be received and expressed in our world. You CAN have what you want. You CAN have your "Good." The Accelerated Method will guide you and set you on your way to manifesting whatever you desire. Oh, by the way, as for me, the fact that you are reading this book is evidence that this method works and I am receiving my good right now.

And as God saw the works of His Hands as Good, so I see you GOOD – VERY GOOD! Be blessed my friend and Experience the Good!

REFERENCES

1   Psalm 34:8

2   Matthew 19:17

3   Matthew 3:14

4   Psalm 37:4

5   John 6:44

6   John 8:32

7   Matthew 6:10

8   Acts 17:28

9   John 10:10

10   Buddha's First Noble Truth is based on "dukkha" – translated "suffering". Dukkha indicates a lack of satisfaction; a sense that things never measure up to our expectations or standards. The emphasis on dukkha is not to be pessimistic, rather to identify the nature of dukkha, so that dukkha things may be overcome. Unless we can gain insight into "Truth" and understand what is really able to give us happiness, and what is unable to provide happiness, the experience of dissatisfaction will persist.

11   Philippians 4:8

12   Hebrews 11:1

13   Mark

14   Psalm 23:1; 37:4

15 Holmes, Ernest. *"The Science of Mind,"* Dodd, Mead, and Company, (1938). P. 64-65.

16 1st Thessalonian 5:23

17 John 4:24

18 Romans 12:2

19 Psalm 139:14

20 Third John 1:2.

21 Luke 6:38b

22 Tracy, Irene. *"The Law of Expectation,"* <u>Science Translational Journal</u> 2.17.2011

23 1st Corinthians 13:1

24 Matthew 10:7